ANIMAL BEHAVIOR

Dog Behavior

BY MARIE PEARSON

Kids Core
An Imprint of Abdo Publishing
abdobooks.com

abdobooks.com

Published by Abdo Publishing, a division of ABDO, PO Box 398166, Minneapolis, Minnesota 55439.

Printed in the United States of America, North Mankato, Minnesota.
052023
092023

THIS BOOK CONTAINS RECYCLED MATERIALS

Cover Photo: Shutterstock Images
Interior Photos: Shutterstock Images, 4–5, 6, 29; Oleg Shakirov/Shutterstock Images, 8; iStockphoto, 9; Thirawatana Phaisalratana/Shutterstock Images, 10; Anna Pozzi-Zoophotos/Shutterstock Images, 12–13; Konstantin Kolosov/Shutterstock Images, 14; Sergey Lavrentev/Shutterstock Images, 16; Aleksey Boyko/Shutterstock Images, 17; Red Line Editorial, 18; Romiana Lee/Shutterstock Images, 20–21; Prostock-Studio/Shutterstock Images, 23; Monkey Business Images/Shutterstock Images, 24; Debra Anderson/Shutterstock Images, 25; DGL Images/Shutterstock Images, 26; Eric Isselee/Shutterstock Images, 28

Editor: Arnold Ringstad
Series Designer: Katharine Hale

Library of Congress Control Number: 2022949103

Publisher's Cataloging-in-Publication Data

Names: Pearson, Marie, author.
Title: Dog behavior / by Marie Pearson
Description: Minneapolis, Minnesota: Abdo Publishing Company, 2024 | Series: Animal behavior | Includes online resources and index.
Identifiers: ISBN 9781098291020 (lib. bdg.) | ISBN 9781098277208 (ebook)
Subjects: LCSH: Dogs--Behavior--Juvenile literature. | Dogs--Juvenile literature. | Mammalogy--Juvenile literature.
Classification: DDC 591.51--dc23

CONTENTS

A dog's body language shows that it is feeling happy.

CHAPTER 1

Don't Hug the Dog

Jada jumped out of the car. She was spending the day with her uncle Mike. He had a big, fluffy dog named Copper. Copper came trotting to her. He looked excited. His tail was wagging back and forth. Jada grinned and put her arms around Copper.

Many dogs do not enjoy being hugged.

His tail stopped wagging. She felt him lean away. Still, Jada decided to pull the dog in for a big hug.

"Jada, Copper doesn't want to be hugged right now," said Uncle Mike.

Jada let go of Copper. She asked, "Why not?"

Uncle Mike explained that dogs don't hug other dogs. So most dogs don't enjoy hugs from people either. Copper had told her to stop in a few ways. His ears went down. He leaned away and turned his head away. The whites of his eyes showed.

Uncle Mike showed Jada how Copper liked to be petted on the chest. Copper's ears relaxed. His tongue hung from the side of his mouth. Uncle Mike said Copper was happy. Jada smiled. She had learned how to be friends with Copper.

To Hug or Not

Not all dogs dislike hugs. A few enjoy hugs. Some like hugs only from people they know very well. But it is always safest not to hug dogs, especially dogs a person does not know.

A fearful dog may have a lowered stance.

Dog Talk

Dogs can't speak with words. But their behavior shows how they feel. Dogs use body language, sounds, and smell to communicate.

An aggressive dog might bare its teeth.

Body language is the main way dogs communicate with each other and with people. People can watch a dog's ears, eyes, tail, and more to understand how the animal is feeling.

Dogs communicate five basic emotions. They show when they are relaxed, excited, anxious, or fearful. They also show aggression. This is when a dog feels it needs to protect itself or something it wants.

Learning more about dog behavior can make life with these pets more fun and rewarding.

People can learn to understand what dogs are feeling. This helps people live safely with dogs. It helps dogs enjoy their lives with humans.

Primary Source

Alexandra Horowitz studies dogs. She explains their reaction to hugs:

> They pin their ears back, they lick their lips (sort of air licking). . . . Or . . . you can see the whites of their eyes. They show behavior that's like, "This is uncomfortable."

Source: Ben Gilbert. "You Probably Shouldn't Hug Your Dogs, Regardless of How Adorable They Are." *Insider*, 21 Nov. 2017, businessinsider.com. Accessed 26 Aug. 2022.

Comparing Texts

Think about the quote. Does it support the information in this chapter? Or does it give a different perspective? Explain how in a few sentences.

Happy dogs may be energetic and ready to play.

CHAPTER 2

Dog to Dog

Dogs have many ways to show their feelings. Dogs that are happy are relaxed. They may wiggle. Their ears move loosely. Their tails wag in big swoops. Happy dogs may dance from foot to foot. They may also give short, high-pitched barks.

A bowing pose signals that a dog is feeling playful.

Playing shows excitement. It is a way dogs **bond**. A playful dog play bows. It gets low in front with its hind end sticking up in the air. Its tail wags. Playing dogs can look and sound scary.

They **growl**. They snap and bite. But their movements are bouncy. They don't bite too hard. They take turns falling onto their backs.

Being alert also shows excitement. An alert dog has noticed something interesting. This dog may suddenly stand still. Its ears are forward as it listens. Its tail may wag a little. An alert dog may become happy. Or it may decide there is a threat.

Talking through Smell

Dogs communicate through smell too. Males and females both leave smells to help them find mates. Dogs can learn a lot from another dog's smell. They can learn a dog's age, sex, and energy level. They can even tell whether it is healthy.

Yawning can be a sign of nervousness.

Friend or Foe?

A dog who senses a threat may become afraid. Its ears will flatten. It may yawn and lick its lips. It may lower its body and tuck its tail. It might **tremble**. A nervous dog might avoid eye contact. The whites of its eyes may be visible.

An aggressive dog has a stiff pose and may jump at another dog.

A fearful dog can become aggressive if it thinks it needs to protect itself. Dogs may also become aggressive if they think something they value, such as food, toys, or an owner, will be taken away. An aggressive dog becomes very stiff and still. It tries to make itself look bigger by holding its head and tail high and stiff, though its tail may wag slightly. The hair on its back might stand up. The dog stares.

Ladder of Aggression

Dogs show their discomfort in several ways before they bite. Helping a dog while it is still showing the lower signals prevents dog bites.

If the threat continues, the dog might growl and show its teeth. It may **lunge** forward and bark. It may snap near the threat. If the threat still remains, the dog may bite.

If a dog is being aggressive toward another dog, that second dog has ways to reduce the tension. This dog flattens its ears and avoids eye contact. It licks its lips. It might roll onto its back. These behaviors show that the dog does not want a fight.

Further Evidence

Look at the website below. Does it give any new evidence to support Chapter Two?

Understanding Dog Body Language

abdocorelibrary.com/dog-behavior

A close connection between dogs and owners can help owners know how their dogs are feeling.

CHAPTER 3

Responding to Dog Behavior

Watching a dog's behavior helps people and dogs live together. A dog's actions can show that it is sick or in pain. Dogs in pain may whine or whimper. They might lick or chew themselves. It may be hard for them to settle down.

A dog in pain may also behave aggressively. This can be because the dog hurts when touched. Owners should take a dog to a veterinarian if it shows these signs. The vet can help the dog feel better. If a dog is being aggressive and is not sick or in pain, owners can have a **professional** trainer help them train the dog.

Training a Dog

Training helps dogs learn how to interact with people. Owners should teach dogs how they want the dogs to behave. For example, owners may teach a dog to sit instead of jump as a greeting. Or they may teach a dog to lie in its bed while the family eats dinner so the dog won't try stealing food.

Training can help address problems with aggressive behavior.

Some dogs may become aggressive if they feel trapped. People should back up slowly and give these dogs space. If an aggressive dog comes up to a person, the person should stand very still like a tree. The person should be quiet and avoid eye contact. This is also helpful if dogs are too excited. They may jump and **nip**. Quick movements and loud noises make dogs excited. Being still and quiet will help dogs calm down.

Relaxed dogs may be open to petting.

People should be careful and gentle when meeting a new dog.

Positive Interactions

Learning how to meet a dog makes interaction fun for everyone. People should approach a dog only if the owner says it's OK. They should avoid eye contact. People should let a dog come to them. They should let the dog sniff them before trying to pet it.

Some dogs prefer playing with toys over being touched.

If the dog is relaxed and happy, a person can crouch down and pet the dog on its side or chest. Leaning over a dog or patting it on the head can be threatening to a dog. If the dog walks away or looks stressed, people should leave it alone.

Some dogs may not like being petted. But there are other ways to interact. With the owner's permission, people can toss treats on the floor for a dog. Or they can throw a ball for the dog to chase. There are many ways for dogs and people to have fun together!

Explore Online

Look at the website below. Does it give any new evidence to support Chapter Three?

How to Approach a Dog You Don't Know

abdocorelibrary.com/dog-behavior

Body Language

Fear

Playful Excitement

Glossary

bond
to form a close relationship

growl
to make a deep rumbling sound

lunge
to jump forward

nip
to pinch with the front teeth

professional
someone who does something as a paying job

tremble
to shake or quiver

Online Resources

To learn more about dog behavior, visit our free resource websites below.

Core Library
CONNECTION
FREE! COMMON CORE MULTIMEDIA RESOURCES

Visit **abdocorelibrary.com** or scan this QR code for free Common Core resources for teachers and students, including vetted activities, multimedia, and booklinks, for deeper subject comprehension.

Booklinks
NONFICTION NETWORK
FREE! ONLINE NONFICTION RESOURCES

Visit **abdobooklinks.com** or scan this QR code for free additional online weblinks for further learning. These links are routinely monitored and updated to provide the most current information available.

Learn More

Garcia, Merriam. *The Dog Encyclopedia.* Abdo, 2021.

Pearson, Marie. *Agility Dogs.* Abdo, 2019.

Tatarsky, Daniel. *How Dogs Work.* DK, 2021.

Index

About the Author

Marie Pearson is a children's book author and editor. She enjoys learning about dog training and animal behavior. She trains and competes with her standard poodle in several dog sports—agility is their favorite—and has helped teach an agility class.